HISTORIC KELSO

A pocket guide for the discerning tourist

KELSO
CAMEOS

Audrey Mitchell

Published by Audrey Mitchell, 19 Forestfield, Kelso, Scottish Borders TD5 7RY. All rights reserved. No part of this book may be reproduced or transmitted in any form or by any means, electronic or mechanical, including photocopying, recording, or by any information storage and retrieval system without permission in writing from the publisher.

Printed in the Scottish Borders by Kelso Graphics.

*Dedicated to all
who love Kelso
Home or Away.*

FOREWORD

Hello, Welcome!

It was a great honour for me to be elected, in June 1998, as Honorary Provost of Kelso and, as a Kelsonian, it has been my sincere desire to do all I can to aid and maintain the progress and welfare of my native town.

Kelso is one of the finest Border towns and very popular with tourists and visitors alike. The Town House in the centre of our Square is where you will find the Tourist Office - a sign of your importance! The town has many historical interests and caters for all ages in leisure, recreation and seasonal activities.

To all visitors I extend a warm welcome for an enjoyable and interesting stay. Whether it be in the town or in the surrounding district, may it be a memorable one!

Best Wishes,

Margaret Riddell.

Margaret Riddell

INTRODUCTION

Sir Walter Scott, who stayed as a boy with relatives while attending the Grammar School in Kelso, wrote of his time there: "..I can trace distinctly the awaking of that delightful feeling for the beauties of natural objects which has never since deserted me. The neighbourhood of Kelso, the most beautiful, if not the most romantic village

*Walter Scott
as a school boy.*

in Scotland, is eminently calculated to awaken these ideas. The meeting of two superb rivers, the Tweed and the Teviot, both renowned in song"... Today, 200 years later, Tweed and Teviot still sparkle as their waters blend together, and although Kelso can no longer be classed as a village, its centre is compact, its Town House still graces the Square and the clock can still be heard chiming above the noise of traffic.

Kelso's name comes from the word "Calx" for Chalk, and apparently there were cliffs with that appearance on the bank of the Tweed, flanking the riverside walk now known as the "Cobby", which is overlooked by a terrace known as Chalk-"heugh" or "height". This area of the town lay midway between Easter Kelso round the Abbey and the vanished Wester Kelso, once sited within what are now the grounds of Floors Castle.

Kelso's known history began at the time of the foundation of the Abbey in 1128 and is linked with that institution until the 16th century. It became a Burgh of Barony in 1634 and developed as a market town, the "superiors" being the Ker family - Earls, then Dukes of Roxburghe. Fifty years later, the centre of Kelso was so devastated by fire that rebuilding was going on well into the eighteenth century.

The railway came to Kelso in 1850 and, although this boosted trade, reluctance on the part of the Duke prevented the industrialisation of Kelso in contrast to other Borders towns. With hindsight, perhaps this was a blessing, as the town remained comparatively unspoiled.

The population of Kelso was fairly static over two centuries at around 4,000 people, with a peak during the building of the railway. Serious overcrowding at this time and the lack of sanitation meant very unhealthy living conditions until a new sewage and drainage system was installed in the 1860s, designed by Sir James Brunlees, a native of Kelso. Early in the 20th century council housing schemes were introduced, providing attractive new dwellings for working people; as these progressed the teeming tenements in the town centre were gradually emptied. Today, Kelso's attractiveness makes it an increasingly popular place to live and the population has risen to over 6,000.

Despite the demolition of many old buildings due to "progress", Kelso has retained enough tangible and visible evidence of its historic past to make a walking tour rewarding. This modest guide is intended to provide you with information for your interest and enjoyment.

Audrey Mitchell, Kelso, 1999.

INDEX TO PART ONE

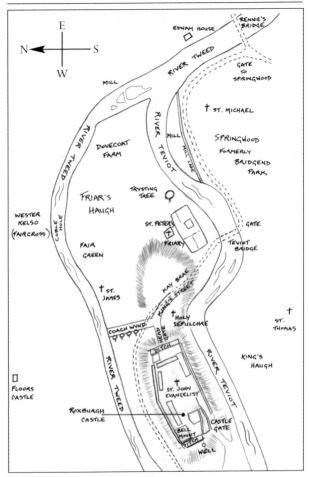

Sketch of Roxburgh Castle and St. Peter's Friary.

Part One

ROXBURGH CASTLE AND TOWN

As Kelso's history was directly influenced by its proximity to the Royal Burgh of Roxburgh, let us begin our story at the site of Roxburgh Castle.

Getting there: Cross over Rennie's Bridge and take the road to Selkirk. You will soon cross a second bridge, over the river Teviot, and about 100 yards further on, on the left hand side, is a stone stile. Over this lies one of the most pleasant walks around Kelso, along the bank of the Teviot.
Follow the path which will take you to the foot of a high grassy mound topped by fragments of the stone walls of Roxburgh Castle.

Sketch of Roxburgh Castle Ruins, c. 1825.

It is hard to realise now, looking at the few piles of stone which are all that remain of Roxburgh Castle, that it was once a mighty fortress. It covered a considerable area, with towers known as the Douglas, Neville, Billop's and Stokhouse which had walls 6 feet thick. Between the towers was a wall, in places 30' high, 10½' thick, with a passage tunnelled through the middle and turrets on the battlements. Inside, dwellinghouses and stables stood against the wall and in the centre was the church of St. John the Evangelist. A barbican or gate-house gave access from the west and the remains of two posterns which once held iron gates can still be seen on the side above the Teviot.

Looking down on the Teviot on the southern side and the Tweed on the northern gives a good idea of the strategic importance of Roxburgh Castle, built by King David I of Scotland in the twelfth century on the site of an older fort known as "Marchmont". Because of its proximity to the border between Scotland and England, Roxburgh was a very desirable possession and changed hands many times. Several Royal weddings took place within the castle walls and King Alexander III was born there in 1241. Henry II of England captured several Scottish castles including Roxburgh in 1174, but Richard Lionheart returned them in exchange for money to fund his crusades. Edward I - "Hammer of the Scots" - invaded Scotland in 1296 and captured Roxburgh Castle. After the coronation of Robert the Bruce, Edward took Bruce's sister Mary as a hostage and imprisoned her there in a lattice iron cage.

On Shrove Tuesday in February 1314, just as it was getting dark, Sir James Douglas dressed his soldiers in black cloaks to resemble grazing cattle on the slopes below Roxburgh Castle. Reaching the base of the walls, they flung rope ladders with metal hooks to hang from the walls and scaled up, surprising the English garrison. However, it wasn't long before Roxburgh was again in English hands, this time for over 100 years.

In recapturing Roxburgh by siege in 1460, the Scots lost their king, James II, for he was killed by an exploding cannon which was trained on the castle from the opposite bank of the Tweed. After this, the fortress began to suffer as it was partly demolished to reduce its importance. Eventually, in 1499, the remains of the castle

Cannon, c. 1460.

and town were gifted by King James IV to Walter Ker of Cessford, ancestor of the Duke of Roxburghe, the present owner. When Henry VIII of England sent his marauding troops into Scotland during the 16th century, attempts were made to rebuild the walls, but without long-term success.

To the Northeast of the castle lay the small but important Royal Burgh of Roxburgh, with the main street, Headgate, running along the rise known as Kay Brae. Tenements of houses lined the route to the Tweed along Market Street, while Senedegate (or King Street) branched off towards Teviot. Two churches, the Holy Sepulchre and St. James', stood outside the castle walls. In living memory there was an annual fair known as St. James', during the month of August, which took place on the site of the old church on the banks of the Tweed opposite Floors Castle. Originally there had been a stone bridge across the river, but this disappeared during the 15th century and a wooden foot-bridge was erected once a year to allow access to the fair ground.

THE FRIARS

Beyond the site of St. James' Fair lies an area known as Friarshaugh, where Point-to-Point races are held. This gets its name from the old Friary of St. Peter which was established here in 1232, with a cemetery dedicated three years later. The order was Franciscan, known as Greyfriars because of the colour of their habits. The Friary experienced the same turmoils as the neighbouring castle and was often occupied by English forces. Edward I lodged there during the invasion of 1296, but the warden showed courage when, at Berwick, he presented a document denying Edward's supremacy in Scotland. In 1460, King James II of Scotland was taken to the Friary, dying of his wounds after a cannon exploded.

St. Peter's suffered with the rest during Hereford's notorious invasion on behalf of Henry VIII and the English soldiers roofed over part of the church as a stable. The last warden died in 1564 and the ground later came into the possession of Ker of Cessford.

Retracing your footsteps, turn back along the road to Kelso until you reach the attractive bridge which spans the river Teviot. Pause here a moment while we discover its background. The bridge is best seen from the Kelso side, where there is a path leading to it.

TEVIOT BRIDGE

In 1784, Alexander Stevens of Edinburgh was asked to draw up plans for a bridge to cross the Teviot, starting from a rock opposite the south-west corner of the Friar's garden. There was a delay before Stevens was again approached in 1788 and

Teviot Bridge.

he produced a plan for a bridge which "shall be executed in a substantial manner furnishing all materials for the sum of £2,495 sterling". The present bridge was built in 1794 according to Stevens' design by William Elliot, architect in Kelso. John Rennie, who later designed Kelso Bridge, was very critical of Teviot Bridge's position at a bend in the river. It certainly wasn't designed for modern traffic! A short distance beyond the bridge, Teviot flows into Tweed with a satisfying chatter of sound.

As you follow the road with the river alongside on your left, you will pass an old mill which has been known as

Maxwellheugh Mill.

Maxwellheugh or Teviot Mill. In 1851 it was bought by the Hogarth family for milling corn and flour and John Hogarth also took over the Kelso Mills in 1900.

The ground on your right, which is now used as a Showground, was once the policies of the small mansion house of Springwood, demolished in 1954.

SPRINGWOOD PARK

The handsome gateway consisting of a stone arch over a cast-iron gate was designed in 1822 by Gillespie Graham for the Douglas family, whose crest of a red heart adorns the centre of the gates and whose coat-of-arms is above. This is almost all that remains of the estate, formerly called Bridgend, which was purchased by Captain (later Admiral) James Douglas in 1750. He built Springwood House in 1756, architect apparently

Springwood Gate.

unknown. James Douglas received a knighthood in 1759 and a baronetcy in 1786. His descendants lived at Springwood, becoming Scott-Douglas after a marriage with the Scotts of Belford, but the family died out during the 20th century. Many family members are commemorated in the mausoleum which still stands on the estate, in a spot overlooking the Teviot.

Several important shows are held annually in the Park including the Championship Dog Show in mid-June, the Border Union Agricultural Show in mid-July and the Ram Sales in September.

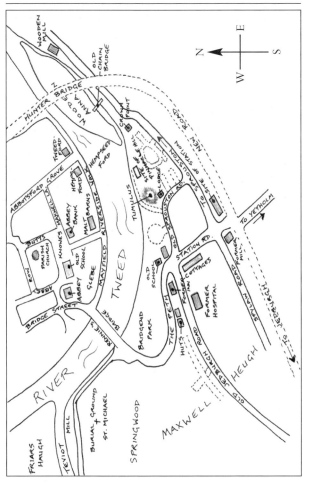

Diagram of Maxwellheugh. (not to scale)

The road climbs a hill after the Springwood gate is passed, leading up "the Peth" to the area known as Maxwellheugh and the former estate of Pinnaclehill.

MAXWELLHEUGH

At the time when Roxburgh Castle was built, King David granted a salmon fishery and land to Maccus, son of Unwin. The fishery became known as "Maccus' wele" and the family, the Maxwells, took their name from the land. They migrated to the Galloway area during the 13th century, but the village still retained their name, adding "heugh", or "height". On the right at the top of the hill is Maxwellheugh Cottage, known as the Abbey Hotel at the beginning of the 20th century. Beyond the Cottage, during the Second World War, there were huts in which German Prisoners of War lived. They were free to roam in the town, but were distinctive in their maroon suits with a large yellow circle on the back.

On the opposite site of the road is the former Cottage Hospital, opened in 1908 and now amalgamated with Kelso Hospital in town.

To the east of Maxwellheugh (on your left as you come up the hill) is the old schoolhouse of the Maxwellheugh English School. Beyond lies the area once occupied by **Pinnaclehill** mansion and farm, of which only some farm steadings remain as part of the Garage. The street names recall the past. The view from the "lofty precipitous eminence", according to Haig the historian writing in 1825, was delightful but is now obscured on all sides by houses. The road on the left is the old way to the village of Sprouston, and some way along it stand the posts of a gateway and a small lodge, the only remaining part of the Pinnaclehill estate. A little gate opposite the lodge brings you to a sloping path which leads to the riverside and a good view of the new Hunter Bridge, begun in 1997.

Photograph of Hunter Bridge opened August, 1998.

To your right as you pass through the gate is a mound, 35' high, said to be a tumulus, or burial ground. During excavations in 1946, three cists were found here, dating to the Early Bronze Age.

Station Road, as might be guessed, led to Kelso Station, built in 1850. Its site across the bridge from the town caused great inconvenience for the population, but considerable income was derived from the tolls exacted for crossing the bridge and some rather dubious arrangements were made to safeguard this. The North British railway from Edinburgh, known as the Waverley route, had a terminus at Kelso and linked up with the North Eastern line from Berwick and the south. Despite public protest, the line was closed by Dr. Beeching's order in 1965.

Kelso Railway Station.

Along Station Road, a terrace of attractive cottages stand on a rise to the right. These were built as part of Springwood property in the middle of the 19th century by Sir George Douglas, the original old houses being demolished to make way.

*Before we stray too far from the town, we had better turn and make our way back. There is a fine view of Kelso from the point at which a flight of steps leads down to **Bridgend Park**, created in 1954 by infill of refuse covered with topsoil. Enjoy a pleasant stroll between the flowerbeds until you reach the bridge.*

Kelso's mediaeval bridges had been destroyed and until the middle of the 18th century the rivers had to be crossed by

Kelso Bridge 1754 - 1797.

ferry, despite the growth of the market town's importance. In 1754 work began on a stone arched bridge across the Tweed, with an access from Abbey Close, next to St. Andrew's Church. If you stand on Kelso Bridge and look towards Floors Castle, you will notice vestiges of the old bridge-end on the right bank below the church. This earlier bridge was poorly built and a flood in October 1797 undermined the third and fourth arches which collapsed into the river. Luckily no-one was injured.

RENNIE'S BRIDGE

John Rennie of Haddington was commissioned to design a new bridge and produced a novel plan for a level road above semi-eliptical arches. Two firms, Murray of Edinburgh and Lees of East Lothian, were the builders and the grand opening took place in April 1803.

The new structure was such a success that Rennie later used the same design for a bridge in London, begun in 1811, finished in 1817, and named after the battle of Waterloo (1815). When Waterloo Bridge was demolished in 1937, two of the lamp standards from it were brought to Kelso and still adorn the Springwood end of the bridge. A plaque beneath the left-hand lamp gives details.

Rennies Bridge in 1825.

At the town end of the bridge, on the left, stands the former tollhouse. There is a groove along the top of the parapet, about $1^1/2''$ from the edge, where people apparently ran their halfpenny coins as they approached the toll-bar. So disgruntled were the townsfolk when the tolls continued long after the building costs should have been cleared, that there were riots in the summer of 1854. Special constables were drafted in and the Riot Act was read. The tolls were gradually phased out and finished in 1857. Beside the tollhouse, notice the old metal plaque giving the highwater mark.

Further along towards the town centre, on the other side of the road, stands the **War Memorial** designed by Sir Robert Lorimer and erected in 1921, after the first World War when 240 local men lost their lives. The names of 41 casualties of the Second World War are also listed.

The adjacent **Memorial Cloister** for the Dukes of Roxburghe and their families was built in 1933, architect Reginald Fairlie. Prior to this date, The Roxburghe Kers were buried in a vault at Bowden, near Melrose; the 6th Duke, who died in 1892, was buried in the south transcept of Kelso Abbey. On this site once stood Abbey House, occupied by the Smith family of solictors and also used as the offices of Smith and Robson, W.S.

Abbey House.

We now come to the most important building in Kelso -

KELSO ABBEY

Opening times:		
April - September	Weekdays	9.30 a.m. - 6.00 p.m.
	Sundays	2.00 p.m. - 6.00 p.m.
October - March	Weekdays	9.30 a.m. - 4.00 p.m.
	Sundays	2.00 p.m. - 4.00 p.m.

King David I (1124-53) was the son of St. Margaret, Queen of Scotland, and inherited her piety. Of the Border Abbeys which he founded, Kelso was the most important and influential. Originally given land in Selkirk, the monastery was transferred to Kelso and dedicated on 3rd May 1128. The Tironensian monks, brought from France, were artistic craftsmen and their Abbey was magnificent, Romanesque in style with unusual double transcepts and a Galilee porch; the nave had 3 bays on each side. Three arches held bells which summoned the faithful to worship and these survived into the 19th century. *The Abbey as it was - drawn by Mr Henry Kerr.*

The Abbey extended from the existing west end to well beyond the old school building, with a kitchen and an Infirmary adjacent where the former Manse ("Abbeyroyd") now stands. Revenue flowed into the Abbey from various endowments, churches, schools and private donations in addition to mills, breweries, farms, granges and flocks of sheep. The abbots of Kelso were important people and often acted as ambassadors, besides having a role as arbiters in local and national disputes.

Kelso Abbey 1825.

Two kings were crowned in Kelso Abbey; James III after his father was killed at the siege of Roxburgh, and his son, James IV in 1488. The demise of the Abbey began as the Reformation took hold and English forces invaded in 1523 and 1545, setting fire to the town and attacking the Abbey.

The fabric was further destroyed by Reformers in 1569 and its beautiful ornaments defaced. The number of monks dwindled and by 1587 they had died out. The Abbey was granted to Francis, Earl of Bothwell, (nephew of that other Earl Bothwell who married Mary, Queen of Scots) Admiral of Scotland, but he was convicted of treason and fled to France in 1593.

In 1602 the town of Kelso and estates of the Abbey were granted to Robert, Earl of Roxburghe. In 1649 a Parish Church was instituted in a building abutting the ruined Abbey beside the West crossing, with the vestry in the Nave. The loft above was used as a school until 1670, when pupils were moved to a new school - one long room with a thatched roof - but still attached to the ruined abbey.

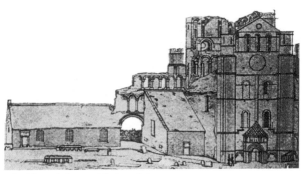

Kelso Abbey with Grammar School attached.

PART 2
KELSO STREET BY STREET

In Alphabetical order

INDEX TO PART 2

INDEX TO PART 2 (Continued)

ABBEY COURT

Formerly known as **Abbey Close**, this is a small cul-de-sac opposite the Abbey, which used to lead to the old bridge.

 On the wall of the second house on the left you will see a badge for the Sun Insurance Co. Anyone who didn't display visible proof of fire insurance was not eligible for the services of the fire engine! In 1802, James Ballantyne was the company's agent in Kelso.

Turret House is one of the oldest buildings left in Kelso. It was built originally for John Palmer, boatman, the date 1678 with his initials above the inner doorway. It was then refurbished for a schoolmaster, James Kirkwood, who was brought to Kelso in 1690 by the Countess of Roxburghe. Turret House reverted to the Palmer family until 1764 when James Robson, a skinner, bought it for £111 and the Robson family retained possession for several generations. Earlier this century three families lived on the various floors of Turret House and older people can remember Katie Bennet's ground-floor sweetie shop, her fat cat lying amongst her wares!

The house was bought by the National Trust for Scotland in 1964 and Kelso's Museum was housed here from 1985 until 1998.

COTTAGE GARDEN TEAROOM
7 Abbey Court, Kelso   Telephone: 01573 225889
Open Easter – End of October 7 days 10.00am – 5.00pm
November/December closed Sunday and Wednesday
January – March closed Sunday, Monday and Wednesday

ST. ANDREW'S CHURCH

The original chapel of St. Andrew was built for the Episcopalian congregation of Kelso in 1769. Following the Jacobite Rising of 1745, Episcopalian worship was suppressed and services in Kelso took place in a room in Woodmarket, with the

Photograph courtesy of St. Andrew's Church.

preacher in an adjoining room, speaking through a hatchway. By 1757 they were allowed to have an English pastor, Richard Wallis, vicar of Carham, and he became first rector of the new chapel. As time passed, a larger church was desirable, so the present one was built in 1869, the architect Rowand Anderson. A small graveyard is adjoining.

St. Andrew's Church is open daily 8.00 a.m. - 5.00 p.m.
Sunday services at 9.00 a.m. and 10.30 p.m.
Wednesday Eucharist at 10.30 a.m.
For details phone the rector on 01573 224163

*The wrought iron gateway on the north side of Abbey Court. A former entrance to **Ednam House**, Bridge Street (see p43).*

Belmount Place

This is the name given to the small row of houses situated at the south end of Abbey Court. At one time there was a path known as "Skinner's Brae" (the Robson family of Turret House were skinners) which led to the toll-house at the end of Rennie's Bridge. The architect Pilkington stayed in Belmount Place while he supervised the building of St. John's Church.

ABBEY ROW

Situated behind the Abbey, this is a one-way street running from Simon Square at the end of Woodmarket, past the Parish Church to the Abbey ruins.

Community Centre

In 1780, the thatched schoolroom beside the Abbey ruins was replaced by a new school on the site of the present Community Centre which stands to the east of the Abbey. This was the brand-new Grammar School attended by the young Walter Scott. The school moved to another site in

Kelso Grammar School, 1780.

1873 and six years later the present building was erected and opened as Kelso Public School. In 1929 it became the Primary School which in turn moved to other premises in 1970. Fortunately, rather than demolishing the building, a new use was found and today the Community Centre is a popular venue for groups and meetings.

Built on to the north side of the School is a burial area known as **Purvis Aisle**, for reasons lost to us. Several people of local importance are buried here and some of the inscriptions predate the rebuilding of the school, suggesting that an old wall was retained.

The church **Burial Ground** is on the site of the original Abbey cemetery and therefore predates the parish church, so some of the stones have 17th century inscriptions. In the 18th century tradespeople such as skinners were in the habit of using the kirkyard to dry their hides and children used it as a playground.

This gave offence to many and in 1807 a subscription was raised to build a wall around the graveyard. Around 1978 it was decided to demolish the wall and create a more open space with intersecting paths. Unfortunately, several headstones were lost in the process.

Old Parish Church

This building, octagonal in shape, was designed by James Nisbet, the same man who built Ednam House. Until it was erected in 1771-73, the congregation had worshipped in the church incorporated within the ruins of Kelso Abbey. There had been a prophecy that "Kelsae's kirk would fall at its fullest", so when a lump of plaster fell from the ceiling of the church at the Abbey, the people decided that it was time to move! The wooden belfry over the North porch was added in 1833. This church, threatened with closure in 1979, was saved thanks to the efforts of the congregation and is well-used today.

Kelso Old Parish Church, courtesy of Rev. Marion Dodd .

Painting of Old Parish Church by **Margaret Peach**
an international portrait painter
and renowned artist of Border Landscapes
Commissions: Telephone: 01573 224236

Old Parish Church opening times:
May - September
Monday - Friday 10.00 a.m. - 4.00 p.m.
Sunday Services 11.30 a.m.
All Welcome

Walter "Beardie" Scott.

The main gates of the Parish Church lead to a narrow road and to the right, on the opposite side, stands an old building once occupied by Sir Walter Scott's great-grandfather, known as "Beardie". An ardent Jacobite, he had taken a vow not to shave until a Stuart was returned to the throne. He died in 1729, still bearded. On the map of 1823 this building is marked "English School", which was later amalgamated with the Grammar School. After that it was known as "Johnny Young's stables". Note the gargoyle high on the wall - affectionately known locally as "St. Simon".

Beardie's House before 1910.

Until 1910 there was only a "stile" giving access on foot from Simon Square (at the end of Woodmarket) to Abbey Row, between Beardie's house and another which was demolished to allow the road to admit vehicles.

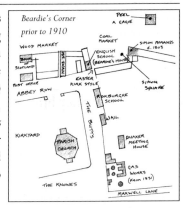

Beardie's Corner prior to 1910

Abbotsford Grove

Running from the roundabout at the end of Rose Lane to the riverside walk at Mayfield, this was known in 1783 as **Thomson's Lane**. On the east side was James Hogg's garden and by 1823 the lane had become known as Hogg's. Later still it changed to **Sussie Hogg's Lane** before the present houses were built at the end of the 19th century and the street named presumably in honour of Sir Walter Scott's home. At the river end of Abbotsford Grove is a ford across the Tweed rather quaintly named "Hempseedford", recalled in the present houses - "Hempsford" and "Tweedford", at opposite corners. "Hempsford" was advertised for sale in April 1851, having two sitting-rooms, two bedrooms, kitchen, pantry, washhouse, water-closet, wine and coal-cellars and an excellent garden. "Tweedford" was once the manse for the minister of the United Presbyterian Church, Rev. James Jarvie who died in 1886. In 1802 there was a fatal accident when a cart crossing the ford overturned and Scott, a meal-maker, was drowned.

BOWMONT STREET

This street, which runs from the gates of Floors Castle to the town centre, was formerly known as Back Way (behind houses facing the former High St.) but in 1892 renamed Bowmont Street after the Marquis of Bowmont, one of the titles of the Duke of Roxburghe. The continuation of the street beyond Trinity Church to the junction of Horsemarket is known as East Bowmont Street, formerly "Caldrigs".

St. Mary's Roman Catholic Church stands on the west side, built in 1856 after the original chapel was burned to the ground by a mob in revenge for the death of a Kelso man, Robert Mills, allegedly at the hands of an Irishman.

Sunday Masses are at 10.30 a.m.
Weekday Masses as announced
Saturday Confessions 6.30-6.50 p.m.

On the opposite side of the road is **Kelso High School**, architects Reid & Forbes, opened in August 1939 just before the outbreak of the 2nd World War. The number of pupils was increased from 693 to over 1,000 by the influx of refugees from various cities. A games hall was added in 1978 and a Music Department in 1994.

Kelso Bowling Club has a green between Poynder Place and Inch Park. In the early 19th century, the Bowling green was at the corner of Rose Lane before moving to ground near Grove Hill. The club was officially formed in 1838 and became known as Victoria Bowling Club when it moved to the present green in 1887.

Membership (ladies & gents) is currently 170. Play takes place between April and September and visitors are welcome. During the season there is usually a presence at the ground should you wish to enquire about joining in, or telephone 01573-226446.

Bellevue House was built as a one-storey cottage around 1846 and became the home of **Thomas Tod Stoddart** (1810-1880), advocate, poet and professional angler, who wrote "Stoddart's Angler's Companion". In his day he was a "weel-kent" character, striding out with his fishing-rod over his shoulder, white beard flowing and dog at heel.

Thomas Tod Stoddart.

His daughter Anna (1840-1911) wrote many biographies, including that of Professor John Stuart Blackie.

BELLEVUE HOUSE

Comfortable en-suite rooms • Quiet location near town centre
River Tweed and Floors Castle • Non-smoking
Private Parking • Pets by arrangement

Bowmont Street, Kelso
Tel/Fax: 01573 224588
Lynn and Graham Thompson

Bowmont Christian Centre has Sunday services at 10.15am (Communion) and 11.30 a.m. (Family) with Bible reading at 6.00 p.m. Tel.01573-223591

Opposite the bus-station is the red sandstone **Baptist Church**, built in 1876 with money gifted by Miss Scott Makdougall of Makerstoun, a very pious lady. She inherited a cellar well-stocked with wine, which she obliged the butler to pour into the Tweed, reducing the poor man to tears as he did so.

Services are held on Sundays at 11.00 a.m. and 6.30 p.m. On Tuesday afternoons at 2.30 there is a prayer meeting and Bible study.

Kelso Library was built in 1905 with assistance from the Carnegie Trust. As early as 1750 there had been a library in Kelso on the Terrace, overlooking the Tweed. Kelso "New" Library, was instituted in 1778 and yet a third, the "Modern"

Library, in 1794. These two amalgamated as the "United Library" in a building at the Mill end of Oven Wynd in 1859.

Kelso Town Council bought two properties in Bowmont Street in 1902, commissioning the architects Peddie and Washington Browne to build a new library in the Scottish Renaissance style. This replaced the older institutions.

Bowmont House across from the Library was a Boarding Seminary for young ladies under the Misses Paterson in the mid 19th century.

Brisbane Place

A small group of dwellings towards the end of Bowmont Street and backing on to Crawford Street. Named after Sir Thomas Brisbane (1773-1860) of Makerstoun, who became Governor of New South Wales in 1821. One of the houses was occupied by the Humble Brothers, famous cabinetmakers, c.1850.(*see also page 52*)

On the corner site below the library stands **Trinity Church**, built in 1886 to a design by John Starforth of Edinburgh. There had been a church on this site since 1750, when part of the congregation of the Parish Church seceded in protest because the Duke of Roxburghe exercised his right of patronage and appointed a new minister without consulting them. The 1779 building which preceeded Trinity was known as the "Riding School" or "Mr. Hall's Meeting House" after one of the pastors.

The congregation of Trinity North was united with St. John's in Roxburgh Street in 1981.

Laying the foundation stone of Trinity Church 1886.

Photograph courtesy of Mrs Anne Scott.

To the east of Trinity Church, **Coldale House** was once its manse and had a garden with beautiful, mature trees which were cut down in the mid 1970s to form yet another carpark.

Across the road, beyond George Henderson's premises, is the Drill Hall, once the **Reformed Presbyterian Church.**

Until 1980, the carpark across from Trinity Church was occupied by "**Anderson's Stables**", a quadrangle of buildings used for horses taking part in Kelso Races and Civic Week. Other stables once stood behind the Cross Keys Hotel and there were two coachbuilders, Maxwell's and Kennedy's, in

D. MAXWELL & SON,
COACH BUILDERS,
CRAWFORD STREET, KELSO.

CARRIAGES of every description made to order of the Best Material, under their own practical superintendence, from the most approved London Designs, and finished in First Style.

Repairs carefully executed on the most reasonable terms.

Advertisement from 1866

the vicinity. The entry between the carparks leading to the Square is known as "**The Dardanelles**", presumably because it was a dangerous spot!

BRIDGE STREET

In the days before Rennie's Bridge existed, this street was known as the High Street. The map of 1823 shows, on the west side of the road beside the bridge, a wood yard owned by Darling and Hume adjacent to the garden of Dr. Wilson's house (now Abbey House) which faces due north. By 1866 this site had been bought by Croall's, coachbuilders and opened as a branch of their Edinburgh firm. Croall Bryson's garage succeeded but relocated at Maxwellheugh in July 1996. A new housing development replaces it.

Croalls Garage in 1914 with former Abbey House in the background.

Moving north along Bridge Street, note the attractive matching detail on the buildings on either side of the road.

They date from c.1870 and may have been part of the preparations for the visit of Queen Victoria in 1867, for she passed along Bridge Street after her arrival at Kelso Station.

On the west side of Bridge Street

The Old Weigh House stood beside the present gateway into Ednam House. Originally owned by the Roxburghe family, it was converted into a dwellinghouse in the early 19th century and later became the "Weigh-House Inn". It has remained as a public house since then, but with several changes of name. Older townsfolk remember carts being weighed and carters receiving tickets on a bridge which was sited in front of the present gate.

No. 11 Bridge St., the shop to the right-hand side of the Ednam House gate was occupied at the end of the 18th century by James Palmer who was editor of Kelso's earliest newspaper, the "Kelso Chronicle". Suspected of having sympathy with the French Revolution, his nickname was "Black Neb". A later occupant was coppersmith William Muir, who in 1822 was the first man in Scotland to introduce gas lighting to his house.

Tweedside Tackle, the shop opposite Ednam House, was formerly a highclass draper's emporium run by the Purves family.

Here you may obtain Trout Fishing permits, Salmon lettings, or hire rods and waders.

According to Stoddart the casts on Floors water running past Kelso are:
the Slates, Blackstane, Weetles, Huddles, Shot, Hedge-end, Shirt-stream, Skelly Rock, Coach Wynd, Income, Cobby-hole, Putt, Back Bullers, Maxwheel.

Ednam House Hotel was built in 1760 on the site of the Chatto Lodging House which had been owned by a branch of the Ker family. It is said that Bonnie

Ednam House as it was.

Prince Charlie lodged there in November 1745 during his journey through the Borders, prior to the battle of Culloden. The small mansion which still stands in this lovely spot overlooking the Tweed was built by James Dickson, who was born in Stichill in 1712, went to London and made a fortune as a merchant and navy agent. Returning to his native soil, he bought land and property in and around Kelso, employed local architect James Nisbet to build Ednam House (originally known as "Havannah House") and the Cross Keys Hotel. Ednam House was bought by the Brooks family in 1928 and converted into an hotel. Fortunately it retains many of the original features, fittings and atmosphere of a delightful residence and still has Dickson's crest in the pediment over the front door. The riverside gardens are particularly pleasant for a quiet evening drink, weather permitting.

(For more information, see "James Dickson & his Legacy" by Audrey Mitchell)

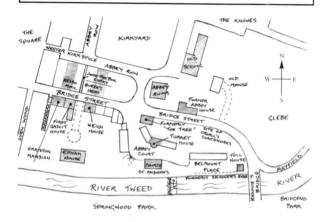

5-7 Bridge St. is a building which once belonged to Charles
Ormiston, a Quaker merchant and banker during the 17th
century. One of his female descendants married into the
Waldie family of Hendersyde and the property became their
winter residence. It was once a high-class draper's - the
porch still has a mosaic floor saying "Commercial House" -
known as Lugton & Porteous. By the 1930s there were two
firms occupying the building, Stempels who had a tea-room,
and Mr. Bews the tailor.

In the 18th century, there was an upper room in this property which was used as a small private chapel for Roman Catholic worship by the wife of Dr. William Ormiston. It was still in existence until recent years.

COMMERCIAL HOUSE,
BRIDGE STREET, KELSO.

LUGTON & PORTEOUS

RESPECTFULLY call attention to the Large and Rich Stock of all classes of Drapery Goods they always have on hand.

They themselves, as well as their Milliner, visit London frequently, and can always give Ladies the choice of the First Fashions in

MANTLES, JACKETS,
SHAWLS, BONNETS, HATS, DRESSES,
SILKS, &c., &c.

Every kind of Millinery and Dressmaking done on the Premises, by Experienced Hands.

Advertisement from 1866

__The east side of Bridge Street__ was anciently occupied by tombs, paid for by wealthy men who imagined that their bones would lie forever undisturbed within the precincts of the Abbey.)

The photograph shows the building which formerly housed the office of the newspaper "Kelso Mail", founded in 1797 by James Ballantyne. He became Sir Walter Scott's publisher, beginning with his "Minstrelsy of the Scottish Border". When Ballantyne moved to

Kelso Mail Office.

Edinburgh, the "Mail" was taken over by his brother, Alexander, father of R.M. Ballantyne, author of "Coral Island" and other stories. Alexander also moved to Edinburgh and the "Mail" was sold to another Kelso family, the Jerdans. In 1856, human bones were dug up in the cellar of this building.

The nearby close which cuts through to Abbey Row is called **"Jock the Box's Entry"**.

The **Queen's Head Hotel** (possibly the head of Mary, Queen of Scots) was once rated for window duty which was introduced in 1695. A large apartment at the rear of the hotel was used to receive aristocratic visitors. In 1833 a Mr. Dixon opened a school for Dancing and Calisthenics in the ballroom. In those days the hotel kept ducks which "swattered" in the kirk-yard!

No. 30 was formerly the **Spread Eagle Hotel**, now converted into flats. The historian Jeffrey mentions "Hardie's Crypt" which occupied the basement of this building.

In 1927 the old horse-drawn bus which took people from the hotel to the Station was withdrawn, replaced by "an up-to-date Morris commercial bus which can seat 16 passengers".

THE BUTTS *(see diagram page 34)*

The Butts lies to the east of the Parish Church, from Simon Square to the main car-park in the Knowes. According to the historian Jeffrey, there was a patch of common here and young men played long bowls on a summer's evening while their elders and womenfolk watched.

Roxburghe Hall in the Butts was formerly a school for the children of the "deserving poor" of Kelso, instigated by the Duke of Roxburghe. It was opened in 1817 and in 1838 was amalgamated with the "Friendly School" whose scholars were in a similar situation. It closed probably as a result of the Education Act of 1872 when all children were given free education.

Kelso Jail adjoined the Roxburghe School on the map of 1823. By 1854 it had moved to Bowmont Street and the Jail in the Butts was used as a police station. In 1905 a new police station was built at the corner of Edenside Road and Rose Lane.

Quaker Meeting House. Where the small business premises are today stood the Quaker Meeting House with a small burial ground in front of it. Kelso had several Quaker families in the 17th century, some of them quite prosperous, but gradually they were absorbed by the established church. The Meeting House was used as a School of Arts and Mechanics Institute early in the 19th century. By 1866, the building was being used by the Congregational Church. The business units were built here in 1970.

CHALKHEUGH TERRACE

This is the site of the white chalky soil which gave Kelso (Calcou) its name. The Terrace, off Roxburgh Street, leads to a fine view of Floors Castle and the River Tweed, with Roxburgh Castle in the background.

The British Legion now occupies the building, opened in September 1795, which housed Kelso's first Library, established in 1750. The librarian lived on the lower floor with a large garden out in front.

Duncan House was used as a school for young ladies, run by the sisters of R. M. Ballantyne, author, for 6 years from 1855.

Hilton Mye was a former manse for the Free Church and at one stage was shared by two ministers, Rev. James Craig of Sprouston Free Church and Rev. Horatius Bonar of the North Church.

Old Photograph showing the Cobby and former Tannery buildings.

Courtesy of Mrs Anne Scott.

At the northern end of the Terrace, by the grassy slope known as the Windy Gowl, stood a tannery business run by the Robson family. There were lime pits, and skins were dried on the slope of the terrace with open drains to the river.

THE COBBY

Now a pleasant riverside walk maintained by the Council, the Cobby is actually owned in sections by the houses above. The wall at the foot of the gardens was built around 1810 to stabilise the ground.

Before Kelso's swimming pool was built, there was summer-time communal swimming, with diving boards and changing huts, at the Floors end of the Cobby.

Once a year, in August, a wooden bridge was erected at this spot to allow people to cross to St. James' Fair on the opposite bank of the river. Boys made good use of the opportunity to swim below the bridge and catch any coins thrown down by the pedestrians.

Photograph courtesy of Lydia Hall.

Until recent times, the Cobby was used as a drying area for clothes and the laundry of the residents could be seen blowing gaily in the wind!

COAL MARKET

Coalmarket / corner of Cross Street, c 1970.

Situated at the eastern end of Woodmarket, this small square was once used as an area for selling coal and cattle. Coal came from Scremerston in Northumberland but was of inferior quality, costing 7d per cwt. in summer or 8d in winter. (The price dropped when the railways began carrying coal). It was delivered in bulk and weighed by steel-yards, then customers could either collect it or have it collected for them by the cart-load. The **Waggon Inn** (now the Horse & Waggon) was used by coal-carriers who took coal from the station to Coalmarket.

Until circa 1820 a very old building, shown on the map of 1684 and mentioned in Stent Masters minutes of 1814, stood in the middle of Coalmarket. This was called the "PEEL A GAGIE" and "peel" is a tower but what might it have been used for......? *(see diagram page 34)*

CRAWFORD STREET

A short street which runs from Union Street to the rear of the Cross Keys Hotel. There was a merchant called John Crawford who owned property here prior to 1750, but it has also been claimed that the street was named after a feu-broker who laid down the conditions for creating it around 1850.

The **Red Lion Inn** is mentioned in a list of traders of 1826 as being run by Thomas Cochran; by 1866 it was occupied by Alexander Buddo. It was completely rebuilt, in commendable Edwardian style, in 1905.

The brothers **George** and **James Humble**, furniture makers famous in their day, in 1832 built a workshop at no. 3 Crawford Street and were later succeeded by Frazer and Wight. This was an attractive building which survived until 1990. Many people will remember the main shop of Oliver Wight which stood a short distance away in Kelso Square.

Chair by Geo. Humble 1825.

In 1866, coach-builders known as Maxwell (see also page 40) had their workshops at the corner opposite the Red Lion. In more recent times they were occupied by Watson's garage until that firm moved to the Golf Course Road. The empty premises were then taken over by local journalist John Dawson, who produced a small weekly newspaper called "Kelso Echo" for a short time from 1983.

The site of these old buildings is now occupied by a block of new houses.

THE SOUND OF NEVE IS WORLDWIDE

THE Kelso Echo

Coldstream : Morebattle : Yetholm
Circulation Area : Kelso and District

THE THIRD GENERATION as Specialists Keeping Time in Kelso
W. J. BLAIR
Watchmaker and Jeweller
The Square
KELSO
Telephone 24736

No. 1   FRIDAY, 21st OCTOBER, 1983.   PRICE 15p

CROFT PARK

"Croft" was the name given to a piece of arable land attached to a farm. In Kelso the "Crofts" was an area to the north of Love Lane, now Inch Road. Croft House stood on the Backway, now Bowmont Street, was absorbed into the grounds of Kelso High School and eventually demolished in 1998. Croft Park, a green area opposite the wall of Floors Castle - "the Duke's Dyke" - and the adjacent Croft Road still carry the name. In recent memory it was known as "farmer Allan's field" and children went sledging there in winter.

Angraflat at the Northern edge of Croft Park c. 1970.

DRYING HOUSE LANE

Running from Shedden Park Road to the roundabout at Edenside Road, this road was the site of a Drying House, not for clothes but tobacco. After the American War of Independence, the price of tobacco rose steeply and Dr. Charles Jackson of Nicolatownfield (later renamed Rosebank) who had been to the West Indies, started to grow his own. Local people (in common with thousands throughout Scotland) followed his example. The leaves were dried in a building standing roughly where the bungalows are today. The government discovered that they were losing a great deal of money in taxes on tobacco, bought up all the produce, burned it at Leith and banned future growth.

Woodside

On the east side of the lane stands a mansion which, with extensive grounds, once belonged to Lady Diana Scott, daughter of Lord Marchmont. She was estranged from her father because his politics disagreed with those of her husband, Walter Scott of Harden. Lady Diana lived to a great age, dying in 1827. Woodside was used as an hotel but has now been converted into flats.

EDENSIDE ROAD

Running from the end of Horsemarket towards Ednam and ending at the junction with Inch road, numerous fine houses were built here by wealthy merchants during the 18th and 19th centuries. The street took its name from **Edenside House** which was built in the style of a classical villa in the late 18th century on the site of an older house called Essex Hall. Edenside was occupied by James Tait, a lawyer and, after his death in 1847, by his son James.

Also in Edenside Road stands the **Tait Hall**, which was built in 1934 with money bequeathed by William Tait of Invercargill, New Zealand, son of James Tait of Edenside House. The site, which was gifted by Mr. Arthur Middlemas, had once been an exercise and training yard for locally-owned racehorses.

The present **Grove House**, residential home in Edenside Road, stands on the site of the High School which was built in 1877 and used until the new school opened in 1939.

Kelso High School 1877 - 1939.

ELLIOTS CLOSE

Off Horsemarket, a small vennel winds past no. 22 and at one time cut through to Bowmont Street. This led to the premises of William Elliot, architect, builder and timber merchant, famous in the early 19th century. Among other projects, he built Teviot Bridge to a design by Stevens.

FLOORS CASTLE

The original building at Floors was very old, a plain and simple house of a type found throughout the Borders. Inherited by Ker of Cessford in the 16th century, it was largely rebuilt by his descendant, John first Duke of Roxburghe in 1721, with William Adam as architect. Much of the building material came from demolition of the Friars, the monastery below Roxburgh Castle which by then also belonged to the Duke. Adam's plain edifice was embellished in 1849 by William Playfair, who added turrets with ogee domes and created the elaborate building which stands today.

Until 1929 the main entrance to Floors was around the corner from the present one, facing the Edinburgh road. In that year the 8th Duchess of Roxburghe, an American heiress, made a 25th wedding anniversary gift of new gates and lodges to her husband. The architect was Reginald Fairlie, who later designed the Roxburghe Memorial Cloister beside the Abbey.

FLOORS CASTLE   *Home of the Duke and Duchess of Roxburghe*

Opening times: April 2nd until October 31st 1999 10.00am to 4.30pm

In the Castle grounds there is a restaurant and a coffee shop which serves light snacks.

For more information Phone: 01573 223333 or Fax: 01573 226056

FLOORS CASTLE GARDEN CENTRE

An extensive collection of David Austin English and old fashioned roses
Herbaceous plants, shrubs and climbers.

Pleasantly situated within the walled garden at Floors Castle.

open 7 days 9.00am – 5.00pm   telephone: 01573 224530

FORESTFIELD

Originally part of Inch Road, where a row of houses is marked
as Forestfield on the map of 1854, the name now applies to
the narrow street which runs from Inch Road to Edenside
Road. This ground, part of an area known as the "Tofts", was
owned by a number of people and was divided into rigs, or
strips of ploughed land. Towards the end of the 18th century,
much of the land was sold to Andrew Lockie who had a
nursery for trees, probably giving rise to the name
"Forestfield". Ground at the western corner on Edenside Road
was used as the kitchen garden for Ednam House, having
been bought by James Dickson at the time he built his
mansion.

Maitland House began life in 1856 as a Boarding Academy
for Girls run by a Welsh lady, Miss Williams, assisted by
Miss Watt. Here the pupils were prepared for courses at
St. Andrew's University and included Jane Stoddart, (1863-
1944) who became a noted writer and journalist. In 1895
Maitland House was bought by James Smith, first Provost
of Kelso.

By the middle of the 19th century, the nursery ground was being sold off in plots for building, and in 1846 Dr. Charles Wilson built his house "Neworth" on the eastern corner of Edenside Road. His report of 1847 on the sanitary condition of Kelso makes grim reading and preceded the cholera epidemic of 1849. In 1853, Dr. Wilson sold up and

Dr. Charles Wilson.

moved to Edinburgh, where he was involved in founding the Sick Children's Hospital.

GROVEHILL

At the point where the "Backway" (now East Bowmont Street) joins Horsemarket, there was an orchard set in front of a detached house, known as "Grove Hill". In 1823 this was occupied by Mr. Lilly, then in 1866 by Mr. Charles Robson, a partner in the legal firm of Smith & Robson in Bridge Street. The present houses were built by Kelso Town Council in 1933.

HERMITAGE LANE

A small cul-de-sac leading from Shedden Park Road towards the river, previously known also as Pointfield Lane.

Two fine houses stand on this lane. **Hermitage** is shown on the map of 1823, occupied by a Mr. Elliot. In 1866 it was occupied by Thomas Fair Robertson of St. Foin and in 1900 by Thomas Boazman, a cattle-dealer.

The site now occupied by **Pointfield**, a small Georgian residence, was a plot of ground purchased from the Rosebank estate. In 1823 it is marked "Mr. William Elliot" and was built shortly after. This house was occupied in 1841 by Captain Pringle Douglas of the Royal Navy. The naval connection continued with the Purves family, when Robert Purves became a surgeon on H.M.S. Captain. His ship foundered in Vigo Bay in September 1870 and Robert was drowned.

At the corner of Shedden Park Road in 1823 stood the property of Mr. Robert Glaister, a veterinary surgeon. Opposite, to the west, was a wood yard shared by Messrs Cuthbertson & Anderson.

HORSEMARKET

This is one of Kelso's main streets, running east from the northern side of the Town Hall to a roundabout at the end of Bowmont Street. Certain buildings on the street have been redeveloped in recent years, although the layout of the entire street remains unaltered since the 17th century.

At the western end, no. 16 was once Kelso's theatre, built by French prisoners during the Napoleonic wars and dedicated to Thalia and Melpomene. The building was converted into a garage and then demolished to be replaced by a functional but featureless modern shell.

The building opposite, nos. 1-5, dates from the mid 18th century although the original would date from the 17th century if not before.

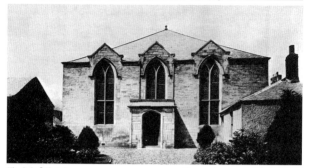

The Relief Church.   *Photograph courtesy of Mr B. Lough.*

The **Roxy Cinema** at the eastern end started life as the **Relief Church**, opened in 1792 under its pastor, Rev. John Pitcairn. His branch of dissenting Presbyterians rejoiced in the name of "Auld Lichts", who reunited with the main body in 1839. Earlier this century, a long-handled pump stood beside the Church and people could fill their jugs with pure water from the Pipewell Brae. The Church, laterly known as "Edenside", continued to be used until 1932 when it amalgamated with St. John's in Roxburgh Street and the building became a cinema.

The Roxy Cinema (Tel. 224609) shows films on 4 nights, with matinees during school holidays.
On 3 nights per week bingo is played here.

W.G. Gilchrist Esq., J.P.
Alison & Hobkirk, Architects,
Hawick February, 1932.

The handsome former **Post Office**, now used as a parcel office, was designed by W.T. Oldrieve and built around 1910.

On the opposite side of the street stood **Victoria Buildings**, with a design of the four suits of playing-cards set out amongst the roof-slates, removed during the 1970s.

At 19 Horsemarket, in the 1930s, the Italian family of Forte had a cafe.

Within living memory, horse fairs were held regularly in Kelso and horses showed their paces by being run up and down Horsemarket. There was Hope's smithy at the corner of Cross Street, a busy place on fair days, and many a deal was struck in the **Black Swan**, over a pint!

INCH ROAD

This street leaves Bowmont Street opposite Winchester Row and runs to join Edenside Road. On the map of 1823, Inch Road is called "Love Lane" and stretches into leafy countryside with no buildings on it. To the north, in the Crofts, lay a marshy area - "Inchmyre" - where linen was bleached before sale.

Inch Road might now be regarded as the locus of Kelso's Health Service.

Kelso Health Centre in 1967.   *Courtesy of Hector Innes.*

At the eastern end, **Kelso Health Centre**, built in 1967 to a design by architect Peter Womersley, received a Civic Trust Award and was extended in 1980. One of the earlier doctors also had his surgery in Inch Road, where a small wooden store faces the hospital grounds.

Front facade of hospital 1985.

Half way along Inch Road is **Kelso Hospital** which incorporates a building dating from 1854, when the Union Poorhouse, remembered by older townsfolk, was built on ground called "the Tannage". The Union consisted of Kelso Parish and 15 others in the vicinity, who all contributed to the upkeep of the Poor House and were entitled to beds pro rata. The regime was deliberately severe in order to discourage any malingerers and families were segregated into male and female wings. In 1948, at the introduction of the National Health Service, the Poor House was converted into a hospital for elderly people and was recently amalgamated with the Cottage Hospital.

If you require medical service while you are staying in Kelso, you may make an appointment or call a doctor by telephoning 01573-224424)

An Accident and Emergency Service is provided at the Health Centre between 9.00 a.m. and 6.00 p.m. Outwith those hours, emergencies are dealt with at the Hospital (01573-223441).

Kelso Swimming Pool Prior to the opening of the Swimming Pool in June 1973, Kelso folk went swimming at the north end of the Cobby on the Tweed where diving boards were erected and families had enjoyable summer gatherings. However, swimming in the river was unsafe and there were several drowning tragedies.

The pool opens at 6.45 a.m. daily and until 9.00 a.m. adults only are admitted. Throughout the day there are swimming sessions for mixed groups, schools, ladies only or aquarobics. You can check out a suitable time to visit by phoning 01573 224944.

Connected with the Swimming Pool is **Kelsac Sub Aqua Club** who have training sessions there on Thursday evenings 7.45-8.45 p.m. Dives are on Sundays. For children there is a Junior Snorklers course. Further information from Andy Wright on 01573-224161.

Kelso North Church was built in 1837 on the site now occupied by the small workshop units in the old school building at the west end of Inch Road. Its first minister was the famous hymn-writer, Rev. Horatius Bonar, who lived in the manse which is now hidden from view behind a  small store opposite the hospital. The Church was demolished some time after its closure in 1940.

THE KNOWES

The large car-park beside the Parish Church stands on ground known as "The Knowes", which means knoll or hillock. Local legend says that the name originates from mass graves at the time of the plague in 1645. During the 19th century, the Knowes was used as a playground for the Roxburghe School in the Butts as well as the Grammar and English schools. Added to that, it was the favourite site for visiting shows or circuses, so a noisy place it could be!

In 1864, a Bronze Age urn was found in a short kist buried here.

Most of the big houses around this area were built at the beginning of the 19th century. The one with the dog above the gateway is Waverley Cottage, known as Garden Cottage when Sir Walter Scott stayed there with his Aunt Janet around 1780, and much altered at a later date.

Abbey Bank was built by Dr. James Douglas in 1815. He had inherited Ednam House from an aunt and stayed there for some years before moving to his new dwelling. Later Abbey Bank was occupied by the Darling family, well-known in banking and legal circles and by Mary Darling after she married James Roberton of Ladyrig.

ABBEY BANK

*Guest House run by **Diah and Douglas McAdam**
quietly located by Kelso Abbey.*
Telephone or Fax 01573-226550
e-mail: diah@abbeybank.freeserve.co.uk
http://www.aboutscotland.com/kelso/abbeybank.html
All bedrooms with en-suite, television and coffee or tea-making facilities.

IAN HIRD

KELSO POTTERY

Ian and Elizabeth Hird opened for business in 1970 and produce a range of simple, practical stoneware pottery.

In 1988 they built the unique Pit-Kiln.

Opening times: Studio and Shop
Monday - Saturday
10.00 a.m. - 1.00 p.m. and
2.00 p.m. - 5.00 p.m.
Telephone: 01573 224027

Kelso Pottery was originally the Gas House, occupied by the manager of the Kelso Gas Company, formed in 1831, whose Works stood to the east of the house. The Company was nationalised in 1949 and production ceased in 1958.

Kingdom Hall at 5, the Knowes holds a Public Meeting of Jehovah's Witnesses every Sunday at 10.00 a.m. with Watchtower Study at 10.50 a.m.

On Tuesdays at 7.00 p.m. there is Congregation Book Study and on Thursdays Ministry School and Service Meeting from 7.00 p.m.

MAXWELL LANE

A narrow street starting opposite the car-park in the Knowes and ending at Abbotsford Grove.

The house known as **St. Leonard's** was built as a manse for the Relief Church in Horsemarket and first occupied by the minister, Rev. John Pitcairn. In 1871 it was the abode of an artist, Robert Frain and 20 years later of Mr. Croall the coachbuilder.

The horse-shoe shaped building was built in 1806 by Robert Nichol, a wine merchant, and marked on the map of 1823 as "Edenbank". By 1866 it had become known as **Maxwell Place.**

Much of the land in this area once belonged to the Rosebank estate, laid out as gardens by the Millers, a wealthy Quaker family of seedsmen from Edinburgh who were connected to the Ormistons, Quakers in Kelso.

MAYFIELD

Today Mayfield is a pleasant riverside walk along the bank of Tweed from Rennie's Bridge to the foot of Abbotsford Grove.

The name appears on the map of 1823 where the ground is marked "Miss Broomfield of Mayfield". There were some buildings known as "Malt Barns" roughly where the older block of flats stands today. They had a chequered history, being used as a barracks during the Crimean War and later the armoury for the Kelso Rifle Company. There was a hospital run by the Parochial Board and in 1899 this was used for infectious diseases. The Malt Barns became a hostel for tramps.

In 1865 the seed firm of Stuart and Mein bought premises in Woodmarket where they built an attractive shop (see p91) with a warehouse backing on to Abbey Row and a nursery sited on Bowmont Street. In 1910 the firm was taken over by Thomas Laing and Robert Mather who developed the famous "Kelsae Onion", using the walled garden of Stichill House several miles from town. Eventually Laing & Mather bought ground at Mayfield for this purpose

THE BORDERS PREMIER GARDEN CENTRE *Tel: 01573 224124*

and it gradually evolved into a general nursery. Around 1971, the firm of Sinclair McGill bought over the nursery and created a garden centre called Mayfield. As it expanded, the premises in Woodmarket and Abbey Row were sold and in 1997 Mayfield came under the ownership of Klondyke Garden Centres.

MILL WYND

Taking its name from Kelso Mill, which dates from the time of the Abbey, Mill Wynd starts opposite the Town Hall and runs towards the Tweed. During the last century, it was a very crowded residential street, full of insanitary tenements, but also boasting the Salmon Inn as well as several shops. When the new Council housing schemes were built, people were moved from Mill Wynd and today it is almost deserted.

Hogarth's Mill stands on the site of the original mediaeval mill which was operated by the monks of Kelso Abbey and a segment of very old wall can be seen at the Dunn's Wynd end of the property. The present office buildings date from the early 19th century when the mill was run by the Broomfield family.

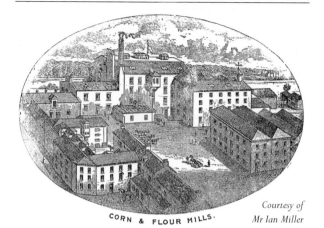

CORN & FLOUR MILLS.

Courtesy of
Mr Ian Miller

Thomas Crosbie was miller in 1866 and he was followed by the Dunns, who gave up the milling side of their business in 1900 to concentrate on their trade as corn merchants beside the Station.

Robert Hogarth had been at Maxwellheugh Mill beside the Teviot since 1851 and was succeeded by his son John, who took over Kelso Mill in addition when the Dunns moved in 1900. He died in 1907 but his family continued to operate the mill and the present company was formed in 1935.

OVEN WYND

Parallel to Mill Wynd, Oven Wynd is a very old part of Kelso as some of the remaining fragments of wall indicate. The far end leads to the riverside and a sloping path gives access to the small island, or "Anna" where the townsfolk

were in the habit of spreading their washing. During the 19th century a well-known pork curing business was conducted by the Smith family in this little street.

Oven Wynd leading to the Anna.

At the end near the river, no. 15 was Kelso's New Library, founded in 1778, one of three existing in Kelso during the 19th century.

PEAT WYND

Another old part of Kelso near the Mill which was overcrowded until the clearance. A lodging-house called Shadrack and Nelson's was always full.

POYNDER PLACE

Off Bowmont Street, just below the High School, is a cul-de-sac which was named after Sir John Poynder Dickson-Poynder who became Baron Islington, Governor of New Zealand 1910-12. He had inherited the ground from his grandfather Admiral Archibald Collingwood Dickson, who in turn was the grand-nephew of James Dickson who built Ednam House.

In Poynder Place there are two sports facilities:
Kelso Tennis Club opened in 1953, playing initially on courts in Shedden Park. A newspaper report of 1890 states that "the Tweedside Lawn Tennis Club opened play for the season on the green in Mr. Rutherford's garden in the Knowes".

> There are plans for future expansion, but meantime visitors are welcome to use the Poynder Place courts at a cost of £8.00 per hour per court. A key is available from Intersport in Horsemarket, or phone David Laing on 01573-224381 during working hours, or 01573-224202 evenings and weekends.

Kelso Rugby Football Club premises and grounds are situated at the far end of Poynder Place and the team colours are black and white. The club came into existence in 1876 and the early games were played in Shedden Park, before moving to Springwood Park three years later. Amazingly, the match against Earlston in March 1879 was played under electric light! The ground at Poynder Park opened in 1908 and the club held their first Seven-a-Side the following year.

Kelso's Andrew Ker in Action.

> *During the winter there are inter-club games which are open to the public and in August the Seven-a-side Tournament takes place.*

ROSE LANE

From the junction of Horsemarket and East Bowmont Street to the end of Shedden Park Road where it joins Woodmarket.

The present Council offices beside the north roundabout occupy the former **Police Station** which was built c. 1905. Prior to that, the 1823 map shows a Bowling green on this spot and it still appears in 1854, by which time the road is marked "Rose Lane", presumably after "Rose Cottage" which stood at the southern end.

The sheltered housing development **Rutherford Square** was built in the late 1970s, when the yards of tradesmen were demolished to make way.

Rose lane before 1970.

ROXBURGH STREET

This street runs from the Square in a northerly direction - the road to Floors Castle and eventually Edinburgh. The old name for Roxburgh Street was the Common Way, the road linking Easter Kelso (round the Abbey) and Wester Kelso (within the present grounds of Floors Castle) and it has been one of the main thoroughfares throughout Kelso's history. Old title deeds of properties on this street give evidence of a considerable brewing industry, with "malt steeps" at various points along the way. In 1723, following several disasters, people with malt-kilns were warned not to kindle fires at night or in high winds during the day. A few of the old houses remain, but much of the street's character has been lost over the 20th century.

Roxburgh Street 1905. On the extreme left of the photograph is the shop of Smith the Grocer which is now the premises occupied by the Clydesdale bank.

The corner of the Square leading to Roxburgh Street is known as the **"Cunzie Neuk"**. Now Cunzie is an old Scots word for coin and there is a theory, so far unproven, that the Royal Mint for Roxburgh was sited here in mediaeval times.

Dunns Wynd Off Roxburgh Street's south side. Possibly named after William Dunn, a baker, in the early 19th century

A **Butcher Market** once occupied the site to the north of Dunn's Wynd. Originally the property of the Duke of Roxburghe, it was sold to a butcher called Richard Allan at the beginning of the 19th century. It had walls around 16' high, a gate which could be shut at night and a well for washing down the yard. Animal carcases were suspended from hooks below shades lined with wood and covered in slates.

Until the 1980s, on the opposite side of the road at no. 9, stood one of the oldest buildings in Kelso. It was owned from 1666 by John Chatto and rebuilt after the fire of 1684. It became the "King's Head" hotel but latterly was used as a lodging-house known as the "Crown Hotel". A vennel leads through to **Jamieson's Entry**, the former gateway to a farm inherited by James Jamieson, surgeon, around 1760.

Distillery Lane

The sign for this lane, beside the entrance to the supermarket, is all that remains of the access lane to Kelso's distillery which was set up in the 18th century. The site had previously been occupied by a 16th century house called "Lang Linkie", the birthplace of William Jerdan, journalist. He was a witness to the assassination of the prime minister, Mr. Perceval, in London in 1812. In 1847 the distillery was taken over by Andrew Middlemas and the firm began by cork-cutting and bottling beer, then producing ale and porter and latterly mineral waters. The firm changed hands and left Roxburgh Street in 1985.

Embedded in the "cassies" in Roxburgh Street, near its junction with Union Street, is a **Horseshoe**. Legend has it that the original was a shoe which was cast by the horse of Bonnie Prince Charlie in 1745 - there was a smiddy at that time just a little further up the street at no. 51 - but this is open to conjecture. The name was given to the electoral ward when the first town council came into being. As each shoe is worn out, it is replaced by another.

Roxburgh House is a classical villa dating from the late 18th century. It was occupied in the early 19th century by James Hume, a writer to the Signet (i.e. solicitor), then in 1866 by a surgeon called Stuart, who called it Roxburgh Place.

Adjacent is the site of the house where William Fairbairn, who became a famous engineer, was born in 1789. Among his projects - the construction of the Britannia and Conway tubular bridges in Wales; he also built iron ships for the East India Company.

William Fairbairn.

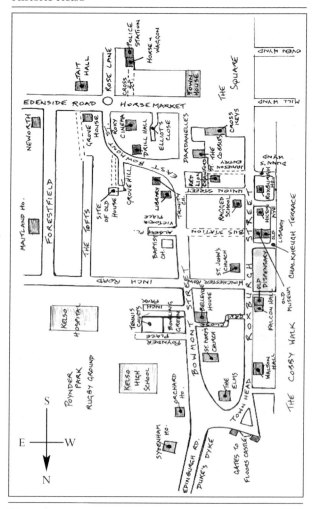

Across the road is an old cottage, gable-end on to the street as many of the houses were, built early in the 18th century (sold in 1763 for £29!) and used for a time as a smithy. The lane was once known as "Hunter's Close" after an occupant who was a nailer. The small cottage adjoining was added later as a dwelling house. The larger house behind was formerly the home of the headmaster of the **Ragged School** (1850-90) and the school was held in the small building on the other side of the vennel which is very old, having a cobbled floor of the type used when animals shared the house! In living memory, until 1973, this entire property was used for a plumber's business by the Makins family.

Roxburgh Street looking South c. 1950.　　　　　*Courtesy of Mrs Anne Scott.*

Kelso Bus Station is the only venue for public transport from Kelso. For information, telephone 01573-224141.

On the West side of the street stood the baths and steam wash-houses which were the forerunner of the Laundrette, drawing water from the Tweed.

The present British Legion building once housed Tweedside Physical & Antiquarian Society's Museum founded in 1834, President Sir Thomas Makdougall Brisbane. It was well regarded in its day, but sounds typically Victorian, with glass cases full of stuffed birds all round an upstairs gallery. Mr. Robert Heckford was the taxidermist. The museum closed and was used as a canteen for soldiers during the 2nd World War.

The imposing church of **St. John's and Edenside** was built in 1866 for the Free Presbyterians, architect Frederick Pilkington.

St. John's Church doorway.

The Church is open during July and August Monday- Friday 10.00 a.m. - 12.00 noon and 2.00 p.m. - 4.00 p.m. Saturday 10.00 a.m. - 12.00 noon. Sunday Services at 11.30 a.m.

Those particularly interested in seeing the interior of the church at a time other than those above should telephone Mr. Cockburn on 224200.

Beech Tent Lane A short lane which cuts through from Roxburgh Street to Bowmont street. There has long been a dairy premises with access from the lane and elderly people can remember the cows in their byres on the adjacent Winchester Row. The dairy is now used for cheese-making.

The **Windy Gowl** is the name of the grassy slope which leads on to the "Cobby" riverside walk. There was once a steam engine and pump here, designed to take water from the Tweed for washing purposes. The tank burst in 1867, injuring a small girl.

Cuckold's Slap is the intriguing but self-explanatory name of the vennel which runs down to the Cobby opposite Winchester Row! At the riverside there stood **Scada Dam**, of which little is known.

The north wall of the vennel forms the side of **Kelso Dispensary**, the house with the classical pillared doorway. It was founded in 1777 with money donated by Mrs. Baillie of Jerviswoode and attended by local physician Dr. Christopher Douglas. Voluntary subscriptions were collected and many people who could not afford medical treatment were admitted to the hospital without charge.

Front door of Kelso Dispensary.

In later years there was a bath, fitted with marble, which could be used by members of the public on payment of a shilling, the money going towards the Dispensary fund. The Dispensary closed in 1906, when the Cottage Hospital was opened at Maxwellheugh.

Next door is **Falcon Hall**, built in the 18th century and once occupied by the King's Falconer, Thomas Barstow. At one stage it was used as a Nurses Home for the Dispensary.

Gray's Close, on the east side of the street, was named after a baker. It was redeveloped in 1960, but at one time pheasants were kept there and the feathers were used to make fishing flies at Redpath's and Forrest's shops.

Walton Hall is at the point known as the "Townhead", near the gates of Floors Castle. Named after Isaac Walton, angler of renown, the house was built by John Ballantyne, friend of Sir Walter Scott. He died before the house was finished in 1821 and it passed to his brother Sandy, father of the author R.M. Ballantyne, who had built "Seven Elms" across the road at around the same time. Over the years, some unfortunate additions were built on to Walton Hall but these have been demolished to return the house to its former happy proportions.

At the Townhead, in 1787, was born William Glasgow. He changed his name to **William Glass**, joined the army and eventually settled on the remote island of Tristan da Cunha. He became its first Governor, dying in 1853.

Painting by Augustus Earle showing William Glass in front of Government House, Tristan da Cunha.

SHEDDEN PARK

Shedden Park in 1867.

Gifted to the town in 1850 by Mrs. Robertson of Ednam House, the park was named in honour of her nephew, Robert Shedden. This gallant young man, despite serious illness, assisted in the search for the Franklin expedition which had been lost in the icy wastes of Canada. Shedden put his yacht the "Nancy Dawson" at the disposal of the search party and her flagpole and two small cannons once stood in the park. Shedden Park has been central to the life of the town for a century and a half and several of its trees were planted to commemorate important events.

(For more information, see "James Dickson & his Legacy" by Audrey Mitchell)

Cricket has been played in Shedden Park since 1857 and **Kelso Cricket Club** was formed in 1861. Between mid-April and early September Border League and friendly games are played in the Park. Visitors are welcome to take part in friendly games, paying a small fee to use the pavilion.

SHEDDEN PARK ROAD

Until the park was formed, this stretch was known as "Bullet Loan", thought to derive from the French word "Boule" for the game of bowls. During the Napoleonic Wars around 1810-15, many French prisoners of war were billeted in Kelso and may well have invented a "jou de boule" here.

There is an old property on the corner of Abbotsford Grove which was once known as **The Academy**, a school for boys, headmaster William Perry.

He had sailed as a surgeon's mate with Captain Cook and went from Kelso to Edinburgh where he started a school but went bankrupt. He wrote a book called "The Man of Business". The Academy under Mr. John Kirkland was relocated to Bowmont Street in 1866. He went to Canada and settled in Fort Frances, Keewatin.

Shedden Park Academy was a later school, on the opposite side of the road and older residents can remember a faded sign above the door.

SPROUSTON FREE CHURCH

In 1843, the Disruption of the Church of Scotland took place and many ministers set up independently as the Free Kirk. The people of Sprouston wanted their own Free Church but were unable to obtain ground from the landowner. Instead, a church was built for them in Shedden Park Road and they ferried across the Tweed to attend on Sundays. Unfortunately the church burned down in recent memory and the building is now unrecognisable, being used as a builder's yard.

Tweedbank is a fine old mansion standing at the end of Shedden Park Road, on the approach road to Hunter Bridge. It was built around 1806 by Thomas Nisbet of Mersington in Berwickshire.

SIMON SQUARE

This Square was named after Simon Romanes, a smith who had the house at no. 1 Shedden Park Road. Simon was killed when he fell from Kelso Bridge while it was being built in 1803. His son, also Simon, died in 1852 in St. Petersburg, where he had an iron foundry. Other members of the family had a foundry in Horsemarket.

Simon's House

Drawing by Lesley Dellow

THE SQUARE

Formerly known as the Market Place, Kelso's Square has existed since the 17th century and probably well before. It has been compared to French townscape and the likeness can seen in these buildings near the Pont-Neuf in Paris.

The centrepiece of Kelso Square is the **Town House**, built in 1816 by the 5th Duke of Roxburghe who had not only succeeded to the title after a long and costly legal battle, but had fathered a son at the age of 80! Originally the ground floor had arcading with gates, intended for market stallholders, but the building was taken over and modified in its present form by the Town Council in 1902.

THE TOURIST INFORMATION CENTRE now shares the ground floor with the Council Chamber where marriages are performed and the fine upstairs room has recently been restored to former glory.

The previous Town House was built by the Countess of Roxburghe in 1696, the year her son Robert, 4th Earl, died in Brussels. By the end of the 18th century it had fallen into decay and was replaced by the present one.

The Square was once surrounded by thatched houses with pointed gables which faced into the middle. (See the drawing on p91) In 1790 the buildings surrounding the Square were rebuilt with the exception of the White Swan, a Coaching Inn. Presumably it was demolished in 1820 when the Commercial Bank was opened on this site. The British Linen Co. opened a bank next door in 1833 and the two formed a fine unit in the style of the existing Bank of Scotland. In 1934, the easter half was rebuilt by the Royal Bank to match its branches throughout Scotland.

Innes Place On the north side of the Square, probably taking its name from Sir James Innes who became James Innes-Ker, 5th Duke of Roxburghe, in 1812.

Kelso Square 1880.

Cross Keys Hotel in 1904.

The **Cross Keys Hotel** was built by the same man who built Ednam House, James Dickson, and finished in 1769. It was originally a stage-post and had extensive stabling, being connected with the Caledonian Hunt and Kelso Races. The facade was radically altered in 1870 by the then owner, James Keddie, and his name can still be seen in one of the etched windows.

(For more information see "James Dickson & his Legacy" by Audrey Mitchell)

THE CROSS KEYS HOTEL
3★★★ RAC AA STB Commended
Mr and Mrs Marcello Becattelli
The Square, Kelso
Tel: 01573 223303 Fax: 01573 225792
E-mail: cross-keys-hotel@easynet.co.uk
Website http://www.cross-keys-hotel.co.uk
Oak Room Bistro and Restaurant

In the Square there is a ceremony each July when the "Kelso Laddie" is presented with his sash by the Provost.

Kelso's Civic Week began in 1937 and the man who was the inspiration behind it was John Scott, baker, Provost at that time. He wrote the song "Kelsae, Bonny Kelsae" which is now part of the annual tradition. The selection of the Laddie is made by the Kelso Laddie's Association and he is presented with a blue flag bearing the motto "Dae Richt, Fear Nocht" which he proudly carries during his investiture.

1937 Provost Scott with Bobby Service, first Kelso Laddie

Courtesy of Kelso Laddie's Association.

There are various rides during the week and a Fancy Dress parade on Saturday to round off the week of celebration.

Before we leave the Square, notice the bull-ring in front of the Town House where the bulls were tethered when the cattle market took place every second Monday, attracting buyers from far afield. An important Horse Fair took place during each March and in July a Wool Fair was held in front of the Cross Keys Hotel. Occasionally a circus would arrive in town and set up the animal cages in the Square, causing great excitement.

Add to this the Hiring days in March and November, when farm servants found employment, the departure of horse-drawn coaches to Edinburgh or London with all the attendant noise and bustle and you will have a picture of activities in Kelso Square during the 19th and early 20th century.

THE TOFTS

Now the name given to a neat cul-de-sac off Inch Road, the Tofts area stretched right along the south side of that street. A Toft originally meant the cultivated ground surrounding a farmhouse, with the Crofts beyond. (See plan inside back cover pull-out)

WESTER KELSO

The village of Wester Kelso, which was linked to Easter Kelso by a road called the Common Way (now Roxburgh Street), stood on a site beside the Tweed which was absorbed within the walls of Floors Castle around 1746. It is known that Wester Kelso was established before Easter Kelso and had a provost between 1165 and 1214. There was a river crossing-point here from Roxburgh and there may have been a bridge. In the centre of the village stood a market cross where King James VIII of Scotland is supposed

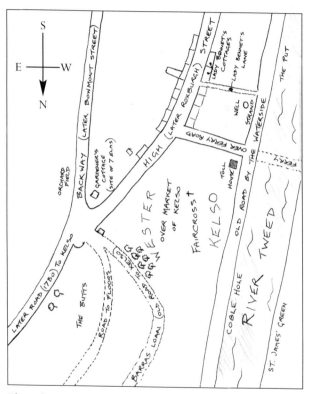

Plan of Wester Kelso

Absorbed into the grounds of Floors Castle 1747

to have been proclaimed in 1715. An alternative old name for this village was Faircross, thought to be derived from "fair corpse", meaning the king's body, for it was here, on a spot marked by an old holly tree, that King James II was fatally wounded in 1460. The site of Roxburgh Castle, which was under siege at the time, can be seen across the river.

Corner of Winchester Row and Roxburgh Street before redevelopment in 1959.

WINCHESTER ROW

Shown anonymously on the map of 1823, this street was later named after John Winchester, mason, who built a row of 3 new houses around 1830. The residents shared a well which is situated behind the houses. In living memory, children who were born north of this point were known as "Roxburgh Street Arabs".

Woodmarket looking towards Kelso Square 1766.

WOODMARKET

The main thoroughfare which passes the south-east side of the Town Hall is marked on the map of 1684 and has always been an important street because it led to the road to Berwick, the main port in mediaeval times when wool in particular was exported to the continent.

Kirk Style is the vennel which cuts through opposite the Town Hall to Abbey Row and, according to the historian Jeffrey, once had a massive flight of steps with a landing in the centre, now hard to visualise. The building at nos. 1-5, thought to date from 1750, has the original shutters on the ground floor and Venetian windows on the first floor.

The building with the Italianate frontage, at present Barclay's Bank, was built for seed merchants Stuart and Mein in 1865, architect James W. Smith.

The old **Bank of Scotland** at no. 25, now occupied by a bookmaker, was built in 1860 by John Burnet senior on the site of the original bank. Kelso's branch of the Bank was founded in 1774, one of the earliest and most successful in Scotland. This bank moved into the premises of the British Linen Bank at the south corner of Kelso Square.

The **Corn Exchange** with its Tudor doorway was opened in 1855 for farmers wishing to show samples of their corn to prospective buyers. During the week there were 67 stalls within the building, but it was also used for social functions including dances and there is a minstrel's gallery inside.

The building known as the **"Priory"** may have been connected with the Abbey in early days, but for many years was occupied by Henry and Robert Swan, "Writers to the Signet" or solicitors.

The last house on the south side has an old **Cyclists Touring Club** badge on the wall, indicating that it was once an approved boarding-house for that fraternity.

Most of the north side of Woodmarket was renewed during the 1970s in a drive to modernise and at one stage the entire row was threatened with demolition. The building at the eastern end of the row was Mr. Heggie's solicitor's office within living memory.

Fortunately the old **Stamp and Tax Office** at no. 22, where official stamping of newspapers or linen was carried out, was preserved. In the 18th century it belonged to John Jerdan, Baillie of Kelso and the building appears to date from that time.

The **Border Hotel** was listed in 1866 as a Temperence Hotel run by Thomas Slight. Mr. Slight was a very musical man, teaching music to the children of the Ragged School and acting as precentor in Trinity Church.

Today the Hotel is run by Ian and Evelyn Galbraith   Telephone 01573-224791

Kelso Crest

OUTER KELSO

On the northern outskirts of the town you will find **Golf Course Road** *which runs from the Ednam road to the Edinburgh Road north of Croft Park.*

BROOMLANDS

To the eastern side of Ednam Road is a long-established small mansion, where it is reputed that Montrose stayed during his ill-fated campaign of 1645. Broomlands was rebuilt in 1719 for John Don of Altonburn to a design by William Adam. It was later occupied by the last Countess of Roxburghe until her death in 1753 after which it became the residence of successive Chamberlains to the Dukes. Now divided into flats with houses built in the grounds, it retains some of the old woodlands formerly known as the West Broomlands Plantation.

Queen's House, at the west end of Golf Course Road known as Angraflat, was originally built as a Fever Isolation Hospital in 1903. The first Matron was Miss Findlater, whose brother was a Pipe Major and a winner of the Victoria Cross during the First World War. The premises were later used as a Red Cross store until 1954 when it was extensively refurbished and reopened as a Home for elderly people.

Kelso Golf Course gives its name to the road, sitting to the north side. It is an 18-hole course where visitors are welcome.

Fees: Weekdays - £14 per round or £20 for the day.
Weekends - £18 per round or £27 for the day.
Details and bookings to be had by telephoning 01573-223009.

Kelso Race Course shares ground with the Golf Course. Horse Races have been run here since 1822, when the Duke of Roxburghe built a handsome grandstand on ground known as the "Berrymoss". Prior to that, races had taken place on open ground at Caverton, towards Morebattle, but it was recognised that moving the course nearer town would bring financial benefits and the traders willingly assisted in the construction of the track.

Racing takes place between October and May each year.

Kelso Racecourse Grandstand built in 1822.

Border Ice Rink, opened in 1964, is near the Golf Club. Here you can skate on Sundays between October and March. Skates can be hired.

Curling takes place on Monday to Saturday during the season.

The adjacent **Skittle Alley** is open all year round.

Abbotseat Bar is open all year.

Bookings for all activities can be made by phoning 01573-224774.

THE LAST WORD

Now that you have been round Kelso and admired its picturesque setting, its historic buildings and its trim appearance, you can perhaps imagine what it must have been like circa 1850. (And Kelso was no different to any other town at that time.)

The houses were mainly thatched and would have harboured a variety of livestock! Windows were usually few, small in size and seldom opened. Many dwellings had a pigsty, some a stable, and the resultant midden or dung-heap against the wall of the house. Although there was a system of sewers, there were imperfect covers and open cesspools which overflowed in a downpour of rain. Some houses had "water closets", but there was no running water and a cart came round in the morning to collect the "night soil", which would have been carried in brimming buckets.

There was a butcher market where animals were slaughtered but many would have been killed in their sties, the noise carrying a fair distance. Dogs would most likely have congregated in the hope of a fine dinner or bone. There were dairies and byres in various parts of town and the cows would have been driven through the streets, adding their droppings to those of the horses. The communal manure heaps were scattered round the town and the sale of "fulzie" was advertised. Tanners had their businesses among the houses and spread their skins in the churchyard among other places. Hotels had stables full of horses and their fodder would have been carted in, the streets littered with wisps of hay.

Houses were mainly located around the town centre, some of them tenement buildings holding many families. There were lodging houses so full that people took it in turns to sleep in one bed, which probably had a bag of straw as a mattress. Cooking would be done on a fire or a range and lighting was mainly by candle or gaslamp. Accidental fires were frequent and caused by sparks falling on thatch or by candles igniting bedclothes or curtains.

Pavements, such as they were, had holes which filled with mud - or worse - and the gutters were so shallow that the walkways were flooded and sometimes impassable. Ladies must have walked with an eye on their long skirts to make sure they avoided the mess and wore wooden "pattens" on their shoes to raise them up a little. In the summertime, streets were so dusty, and odours from the sewers so bad, that windows had to be kept shut. No wonder that people who could afford to build new houses made sure that they were well away from the "noisome" and noisy town centre!

We who are lucky enough to be alive now and not in the "good old days" can enjoy our clean environment and comparative quiet. Nevertheless, our lives are richer for the efforts of those patrons, masons and architects whose buildings we still admire, the skills of the engineers who created bridges and efficient sanitation and the inventiveness of those who discovered gas, electricity and the mixed blessing of the internal combustion engine! May we leave a legacy as beneficial to our children.

INDEX

PLACES TO STAY

BED AND BREAKFAST

PLACES TO WORSHIP

PLACES TO EAT

SPORTS FACILITIES

With support from

THE ARCHITECTURAL HERITAGE SOCIETY OF SCOTLAND

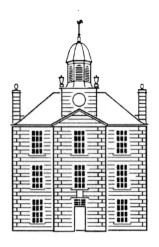

FOR THE STUDY AND PROTECTION OF SCOTTISH ARCHITECTURE

The Glasite Meeting House,
33 Barony Street,
Edinburgh EH3 6NX

Tel: 0131 557 0019
Fax: 0131 557 0049
e-mail: glasite@ahss.org.uk

Membership enquiries welcome